THE CAMPER COOKIE

EASY RECIPES AND COOL TIPS FOR
YOUR CAMPERVAN LIFE

SUMMER BOURNE

So sorry... I wanted this book to have lovely colour photos of the food for you but, unfortunately, it would have made the book a price that I felt was unreasonable. Hopefully you can still enjoy it as it is and still make some yummy food for your campervan life.

While the author has made all reasonable efforts to ensure that the information contained in this book is accurate and up to date at the time of publication, anyone reading this book should note: Nutrition knowledge is constantly changing and the author cannot guarantee the accuracy or appropriateness of the contents of this book.

ISBN~13: 978~1535271868

ISBN~10: 1535271868

Let Me Take You on a Magical Adventure...

Picture this: You (and probably your partner/family/friends) are driving back to your campsite in your campervan at the end of a pretty wonderful day, tired but happy.

This morning you got up early and cooked a delicious breakfast next to your van – boy did that bacon smell good! You then quickly washed up and packed away and hopped in to the van for the day's adventures.

Sense of Freedom

You have a rough plan for the day but you know that if you should find something more interesting to do along the way (or you find a place that is so special you just can't leave it) you can change your plan and just follow your bliss. You are loving this sense of freedom and the feeling that you can go wherever you want.

For the morning you decide to head off to a beach you know as it has a beautiful coastal walk which you are going to enjoy again. But before you set off on your walk you have a coffee in that cute, beach café near the car park.

Somewhere a Little Magical

You do your walk, the weather and the views are amazing, and you arrive back at the van starving. You open up the van and make yourself a chunky sandwich and have a cup of tea and a biscuit before setting off for new territory – somewhere a little magical that you have never been to before but you've checked it out on the internet and you are excited about going there. It is an ancient stone circle on some wild moorland in the West Country. You get there, park up and walk to the circle, taking in the atmosphere of this enchanted land and feeling the wildness of this place. You get to the stone circle and wonder why our ancestors put so much effort in to building these mysterious places and you say hello to a few other travellers who have also come to visit the circle. You sit for a while and enjoy the peace.

Before long, you can feel that the day has reached that moment when it starts to slowly wind down and you walk contentedly back to your campervan.

Relax by the Van

You drive back to your campsite, chatting about the day's adventures, looking forward to relaxing next to the van with a delicious meal and a beer or two before climbing in to bed and sleeping the best sleep you have had in a long time.

This is campervan life and it's bloomin' marvellous...

Why I Wrote this Book

Although I have always been a keen home cook and I am very interested in nutrition, I never thought that I would ever write a recipe book. I always thought that you had a to be a top chef with years of professional cooking to do a recipe book, and I certainly admire those people (love you, Jamie Oliver!). But when my partner Glyn and I got a campervan I realised that fancy, and sometimes even 'normal', ways of cooking just weren't possible in a campervan (or tent) kitchen.

Challenge to Find Recipes

Having used nutrition to recover from a serious, long~term illness, I am now passionate about eating real food and I wanted to be able to carry on cooking real food in our micro campervan. Our camper is a converted Toyota Previa (Trev-the-Prev) and our kitchen is very basic so it was quite a challenge to find recipes that would work easily in this environment. It had to be possible to cook everything on 2 gas rings and/or a BBQ.

As time went on, I found that I was starting to develop my own collection of recipes (or adapting other recipes) for when we were away in the campervan and that I was also cooking them at home as they were so easy, quick and fun.

Why Not Share the Recipes with Other Campers?

I then thought, if we are having to find special recipes for our campervan life, then probably other campers, campervanners and caravanners are finding the same thing so why not write a recipe book especially for them. (My Dutch friends who are keen sailors tell me it is the sort of thing they need when they are on their boat, too).

So here is my first offering of recipes for the camping life. I hope you enjoy it, both when you are out on your adventures, and on a busy weekday night when you just want to cook something easy.

Camping is a fantastic way to see the world and I hope that my recipes can make it just a little bit more fun for you and your family.

Big Hugs

Summer

The Camper Cookie

Table of Contents

Happy Camping and Yummy Cooking

I love camping! Every Spring I can't wait to get out and about in our campervan, 'Trev-the-Prev', to see new places, enjoy nature and generally lap up that wonderful sense of freedom you get when you are in a campervan (or tent, or caravan). As you are reading this I guess that you feel the same way too.

However, I also like nice food and I believe in giving our bodies good nutrition in a simple and homely way. But how do you combine the two? **How can you cook good food in your campervan when you have a limited kitchen and you want to spend most of your time out having adventures anyway?**

Eating Out gets Expensive

Of course, one solution is to eat out and Glyn and I do love coming across a quirky café for lunch or a cosy, country pub for supper, but it gets expensive if you do it all the time. Also, sometimes it's nice to just relax by the van or tent at the end of the day, especially if you **find a beautiful view where you can watch the sun go down.**

Since getting our campervan (a converted Toyota Previa) a few years ago, I have been experimenting with ways to cook tasty food under the sort of restrictions you might have in a small campervan or tent. Restrictions like:

- Limited cooking facilities (often only two rings and maybe a barbeque)

- Limited storage space

- Limited cooking space

- Limited equipment and gadgets (no food processor, blender etc.)

- Limited time

- Limited fuel (especially if you are wild camping)

Great for Week-Day Meals Too

Along the way I discovered some yummy recipes that I cook at home too simply because they are so good. These recipes are not fancy, but they are quick and satisfying in a homely way and are great for a week~day meal when you have come in from work and just want to cook something easy.

Most of the recipes take under 20 minutes to do and many take even less.

I have also taken advantage of some of the **amazing 'done-for-you-already' products** that are in the supermarkets now such as: a packet of chilli spice mix, fruit coulis in a bottle and chargrilled peppers in a jar. They are such good quality and mean that you can bring an extra dimension to your campervan cooking that would really not be possible otherwise.

I have tried to make sure that the recipes are nutritious as well as tasty although they are not meant to be health food or any kind of diet.

You'll also find that I've purposely NOT put lots and lots of different recipes in this book. If you are like me, when you get a new cook book you scan through it and maybe try out half a dozen recipes and eventually cook only one or two of them regularly from then on. So, in 'The Camper Cookie' book, I have given you an interesting range of recipe blueprints that I know work well and then a few variations on the theme that you can try depending on what you have in the van or can buy locally. I would also encourage you to experiment and develop your own versions of these blueprints.

Also, when you are cooking whether that's in your campervan or at home, I would really encourage you to enjoy it and not worry about it being perfect. That's not to say that I don't admire those highly-skilled chefs who put a lot of effort in to making meals that are out-of-this-world. I've been lucky enough to eat at some restaurants where the food is made to this standard and it really is on another level.

However, that's not what we are trying to achieve here; we are just making tasty, nutritious meals in a minimal kitchen with minimal fuss. So relax and have fun!

The Capsule Larder

In this book I also introduce you to the 'capsule larder' concept. Most people have heard of the 'capsule wardrobe' idea in which you have a few items of clothing that you can mix-and-match to give you a whole range of different outfits. Well, I have done the same with cooking ingredients so that you can get lots of different meals out of just a few ingredients and I have given you a sample capsule larder menu that will give you all the tasty meals you need for a 3-day trip (and beyond).

Try at Home First

I would encourage you to try these recipes at home first and get used to them a little before you cook them in the van. It's always easier to learn a new recipe in a familiar kitchen and, as I said above, you may find that some of them become favourites for meals at home anyway. (Shall I tell you something daft that I sometimes do when I am cooking these recipes at home?   I serve them up on our plastic, camping plates so that I can pretend that we are out camping. Silly, I know, but fun!)

Cool Tips that Make Life Easier

In this book I also offer you some tips about gadgets that make life easier for cooking in a campervan or tent that I have learned along the way. And I tell you a little about the nutrition in the food that you are eating so that you will know the good that you are doing for your body as you eat this food.

Watch the Recipes on Your Phone

To make it easier to follow the recipes while you are out and about I have cooked some of them for you on YouTube so that you can follow along on your phone or laptop rather than carry a book with you if that is your preference (and I'll keep adding more).

So please enjoy and I wish you happy camping, yummy cooking and amazing adventures.

Please check out my blog for the latest recipes, tips, magical places and updates on our adventures at www.thecampercookie.com

The Capsule Larder

In a campervan (or tent/caravan) you are limited for storage space and it helps on fuel costs to try and keep the van as light as possible.

So you want to keep your food larder as small as you can yet get as many different meals out of the ingredients that you are carrying (or find along the way). This is where the Capsule Larder idea works so well.

Many of you (especially the ladies) will have come across the concept of the capsule wardrobe – where you have a few key items of clothing that you mix and match to make lots of different outfits. You can do the same with your food with just a little planning.

Make the Most of Leftovers

The Capsule Larder concept also includes making the most of any leftovers, for example:

~ Leftover Chilli con Beanie is brilliant cooked inside a quesadilla the next day with a little grated cheddar cheese and served with a salad. You can do the same with leftover Ranch Beans.

~ Leftover Pasta Genovese makes a nice cold side dish with your BBQ'd meat or fish the next day.

~ You can put some leftover chicken curry pieces in a wrap or toasted sandwich or, thin it down and make a chunky spicy soup.

You get the idea!

Get Your Ingredients to Multi-Task

There are some ingredients that are just brilliant at working in lots of different recipes, things like cheese, eggs, yoghurt, sauces, salad, fruit.

For example:

1. A **Blue Cheese** can go in:

   o Toasted sandwiches

   o Wraps

   o Risottos

   o Breakfast muffins

   o Quesadillas

   o Salads

2. **Eggs** can be used for:

   o Pancakes

   o French toast

   o Breakfasts (fried/poached/scrambled)

   o Salads

   o Curries

   o Sandwiches (egg mayo)

3. **Bananas** can be:

   o mashed on breakfast muffins

   o BBQ'd for dessert

   o a portable snack

   o on top of granola for breakfast

4. **Chicken Breasts** are useful for:

- o salads
- o risottos
- o sandwiches (toasted or untoasted)
- o Pan-frys
- o kebabs
- o curries

It is a whole different way of thinking about food and, not only does it save space, it also saves money and you might find that some of the ideas will work for the way you shop at home too.

I have put together a sample menu for a long weekend that you can try and then adapt it to your taste.

Sample Menu – 3 Days

Here is a menu that you could use for 3 Days in the van. I have put the ingredients that repeat themselves in the brackets so you can see how you can get a lot of 'mileage' out of the same food item.

Day 1

Breakfast

• Stack Pancakes with Maple Syrup (EGGS/YOGHURT)

(Cook up some 10-10 Chicken while you are doing breakfast and keep in the fridge)

Lunch

• Toasted Sandwich with shredded 10~10 Chicken, Sweet Chilli Mayog & rocket (CHICKEN/SWEET CHILLI SAUCE/ YOGURT/MAYONNAISE/ROCKET)

Supper

• BBQ Burger served with Green~Bean & Mango Rice & Geetas Chilli Chutney (BURGER/GEETA'S CHUTNEY/GREEN BEANS/TINNED MANGO)

(Cook up an extra burger for Ranch Beans next day)

Dessert

• Bananas & Custard (BANANAS)

Day 2

Breakfast

• Ranch Beans (LEFTOVER BURGERS)

Lunch

• Eat Out

Supper

• Pasta Genovese & salad (GREEN BEANS/PESTO SAUCE/ROCKET)

Dessert

• Fruit Yogam (YOGHURT/MANGO/BISCUITS)

Day 3

Breakfast

• Stack Pancakes (using leftover batter) with yogurt, maple syrup, chopped bananas & mango (YOGHURT/BANANAS/TINNED MANGO)

(Hard~boil some eggs while you are doing breakfast for lunch later)

Lunch

• Wrap filled with Egg Mayog (use eggs cooked at breakfast) & leftover Geeta's Chilli Chutney. (EGGS/YOGHURT/MAYONNAISE/GEETA'S CHUTNEY)

Supper

    • Pan~Fry remains of 10~10 Chicken and serve with Sweet Chilli Mayog & cold, leftover, pasta Genovese and a Rainbow Micro Salad (CHICKEN/SWEET CHILLI SAUCE/YOGHURT/MAYONNAISE/GREEN BEANS/PESTO SAUCE)

Dessert

• Biscuits and Hot Chocolate (BISCUITS)

Obviously, there is a lot of food going on here and you may find that you stretch this menu out over 4 days (make sure that leftover items are kept in the fridge) or you may miss out some meals and eat out instead. But you get the idea.

*If you are **gluten-intolerant** you can use gluten-free flour in the pancakes and use gluten-free bread/wraps/pasta which are now available in most supermarkets or health-food shops. For the Fruit Yogam you can use granola (if you're OK with oats), crumbled meringues or gluten-free biscuits for the base.*

Staples for Your Larder

Over time I have found that there are few items that I like to always have in my larder and I thought I would share them with you ~ some are pretty obvious but there might be a few new ideas for you. I tend to scale everything down so I am always on the lookout for micro pots/jars/Tupperware containers.

• Salt

• Pepper

• Oil for cooking (Make sure you get a container that seals well)

• Spice of choice for pan-fry recipes and dressings e.g. cumin, Garam masala, Ras al hanout

• Cinnamon (can't live without my cinnamon!)

• Packets of instant custard

• Baked beans

• Maple syrup (Make sure you have a secure container. I had one bottle leak everywhere – OMG never again!)

• Trail mix (great for when you can't get to food but are starving)

• Rice

• Couscous

- Buckwheat

- Honey (can't live without my honey)

- Mayonnaise

- Eggs

- Sweet Chill sauce

- Pesto sauce in jar

- Dried pasta

- Packets of Chilli con Carne spice mix

- Curry Kit

- Chocolate Spread (e.g. Nutella) for hot chocolates

- Brandy (small plastic bottle for chilly-night hot chocs)

- Tortillas (for lunch wraps or quesadillas)

- Mango in tin

- Shop-bought Fruit Coulis e.g. mango & passionfruit, raspberry. (I put a small amount in to a micro jar from the small containers that I have at home)

So What Sort of Kitchen Kit Do You Need for a Campervan?

If you have been having adventures in a campervan for a few years you will probably have your kitchen kit down to a fine art by now but, for those of you who are new to campervanning/camping, here is what I have found really useful for my kitchen kit. As Trev-the-Prev is a micro camper I have to get most of my small kit in to one storage box but it seems to work well. However, if you have a deluxe camper you will be able to fit a bit more in.

Main Kit

- Frying pan

- Saucepan (or two)

- Hubcap grill

- Collapsible kettle

- Portable gas ring (so that you can cook outside when you want to if your cooker is fixed in the van)

Dining Ware

- Knives, forks and spoons (you will need more teaspoons than you think!)

- One dinner plate each

- One side plate each

- One dish each

- Two mugs each (so that you can offer other lovely camping people a cup of tea!)

- One beaker each

Cooking Ware

- Large kitchen knife (buy the ones that have a sleeve for the blade)

- Small kitchen knife

- Micro whisk

- Bottle opener

- Small chopping board

- Fish slice

- Draining spoon

- Pot stirrer

- Small metal kebab sticks (try and get the ones with silicone handles)

- Silicone lids (don't forget the little ones for your mugs)

- Collapsible bowls

- Collapsible colander

- Small cheese grater

- Potato peeler

- Can opener

- Small pair of scissors

- Small tongs

- Sealer-top for wine bottles

General Stuff

•Small freezer bags

•Plastic closers for freezer bags

•Wet wipes

•T-towel

- Microfibre hand towel

•Small plastic rubbish bags

I know it looks like a lot but you'll be surprised how much of the small kit you can get in to just one plastic storage box. As time goes on you might find that you are not really using some of it depending on your camper lifestyle so you can take that out.

Breakfasts

The Beans

Baked beans are a really useful thing to have in the campervan and are especially good with a cooked breakfast. However here is a recipe that gives them a bit of a make-over. It keeps you going until lunch time and you can pretend that you are a cowboy out on the range at the same time!

Ranch Beans

Ingredients (serves 2)

- 1 x 415g can baked beans

- 200g (or half a packet) of meatballs (or a few cooked meatballs/crumbled burgers or chopped sausages from previous night's BBQ)

- 1~2 tbsp of ready-made sweet barbeque sauce

How to Cook

~ Chop or pull the meatballs in to quarters

~ Fry them in a frying pan over medium heat until they are cooked through (about 5-10 mins). You don't need any fat as they make their own.

~ Drain any fat from the pan

~ Empty the beans in to a pan with the meatballs

~ Stir in the barbeque sauce

~ Serve on toast or with a poached/fried egg

Ranch Beans

Make~Life~Easier Tip: If you have any leftovers it is nice with grated cheddar cheese in a quesadilla the next day.

Kit Tip: Wet Wipes

Have a packet of Wet Wipes next to you when you are cooking outside so that you can easily clean your hands while you are prepping the food. However always wash your hands properly after handling meat or fish.

The French Toast

French toast is a great way to use up some older bread as this recipe works better with bread that is a day or two old. You can also make it with crumpets. The eggs give you a good protein hit and keep you satisfied for longer which is really helpful if you have a full-on morning of surfing, cycling or hiking.

Fluffy French Toast

Ingredients (serves 2)

- 2 eggs
- 3 tbsps milk
- 1 tsp cinnamon
- 2 thick slices of older bread (or 2 crumpets)
- knob of butter or spray of light oil (like rapeseed)

How to Cook

~ Whisk the eggs, milk and cinnamon in a bowl

~ Put the egg mixture in a shallow bowl or deep plate and place the bread in the mixture so that it can soak it up (only takes a couple of minutes). Turn it over and leave it to soak for another minute or two

~ Melt the butter in a large frying pan (or spray the oil)

~ Carefully lift the bread with a fish slice in to the pan and let it cook until it is browned on one side, then flip over and brown the other side

Serve with maple syrup or a bottled fruit coulis (the raspberry one is particularly good). You can also try the fruit compotes in jars in the supermarkets now (cherry works well).

Fluffy French Toast & Maple Syrup

Here is another version of French Toast using a wrap and it's from Kim Lee, a recipe developer in the USA who blogs as *'Kim's Cravings'*.

CINNAMON FRENCH TOAST WRAP

Ingredients (serves 1)

- 1 large wrap

- 2 eggs

- 1 tsp cinnamon

- ½ tsp vanilla extract

- optional topping and filling ingredients; such as diced banana, diced strawberries, blueberries, maple syrup, nut butter, shredded unsweetened coconut

How to Cook

~ Heat a large frying pan over medium~high heat and prepare it with an all-natural cooking spray or coconut oil.

~ Whisk eggs, cinnamon and vanilla together in a shallow bowl. Dip wrap in shallow bowl, making sure to cover the entire wrap with the egg mixture. There will be leftover egg mixture.

~ Lay the wrap flat on the pan and cook for about 2-4 minutes on each side.

~ Transfer wrap to a plate and use the same heated

pan (you may need more cooking spray or oil) to cook up the leftover egg mixture, omelette style. Cooking your egg omelette or pancake style makes the egg easier to transfer to your wrap and it also will stay put in the wrap better.

~ Add in all of your favourites, like the suggested banana, strawberries, blueberries and a drizzle of nut butter.

~ Roll up your Cinnamon French Toast Wrap and cut in half, if desired. I added a drizzle of maple syrup and a sprinkle of shredded unsweetened coconut over the top.

Nutrition Tip: As well as tasting great, cinnamon is an amazing superfood. Not only does it help balance your blood sugar (great for stopping the energy dip mid-morning) it is also a powerful anti-oxidant which means it helps keep us healthy and youthful. What's not to like!

The Pancake

I warn you, these pancakes are addictive! They are the sort of spongy pancakes that you normally have for breakfast but we have them as a treat at any time of the day. I also cook these a lot at home as they are really quick and great when you just need something sweet and comforting.

Stack Pancakes

Ingredients (makes 6~8 pancakes)

- 100g self-raising flour (approx. 6 heaped tbsp). You can use gluten-free flour if you are gluten intolerant.

- 1 tsp baking powder

- 225g natural yoghurt (around half a large pot)

- 4~6 tbsp milk

- 1 egg

- ½ tsp vanilla essence (optional)

How to Cook

~ Put all of the ingredients in a bowl and mix until smooth

~ Add a little light oil to a frying pan on medium heat

~ Drop 2-3 tbsp of the batter mixture in to the pan

~ Cook for about 2 mins until little bubbles start to appear and pop on top of the pancake

~ Flip over and cook for another minute or two

~ Remove and serve or keep warm in silver foil and tea towel until you have the stack you want.

For Toppings:

• Just maple syrup

• Crispy bacon & maple syrup (yes, it really does work!)

• Yoghurt, maple syrup and fresh blueberries/banana (vanilla yoghurt works particularly well)

• Yoghurt and any fresh fruit that you like (you could use some leftover fruit from the Fruit Kebabs from the previous night's BBQ)

• Mashed banana & Nutella (now we're getting naughty...)

Stack Pancakes

Make~Life~Easier Tip: *If you are going away for only 2 or 3 days, you can make the batter at home before you go and take it with you in a secure container in the fridge. Give it a good stir before you use it and you may need to add a little more milk to just loosen it off after it's been sitting for a while. Alternatively, you can measure out the dry ingredients (the flour and baking powder) in to a freezer bag and take this with you so that you only need to add the wet ingredients when you are cooking in the van)*

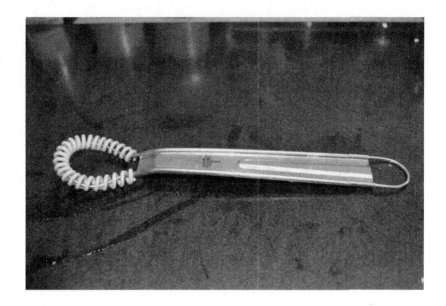

I know it's a bit sad to be so excited by something like a whisk but I love these flat, silicone whisks.

They are small, light and come in pretty colours (Yay!) but they are really helpful if you are mixing up sauces or anything with eggs in them.

They make a big difference in recipes like 'Stack Pancakes' and 'French Toast' and any salad dressings that you are throwing together. You can buy them on eBay and Amazon just search 'Colourworks 21cm Silicone magic whisks. You can often find them in the kitchenware department in garden centres too.

The Granola

A granola is basically a kind of toasted muesli which you bake in the oven so you won't be able to make it out in the van. However, you can make up a batch at home before you go (See 'Tim's Just-Too-Tasty Granola' in the Bake-Before-You-Go section). It's always nice to have a supply at home anyway as a healthy, filling breakfast.

If you don't feel like making your own granola there are plenty or good ones available in the supermarkets now.

Below is my super-deluxe version of a granola breakfast.

Gorgeous Granola

Ingredients (per person)

- 1 bowl of granola

- milk to cover (coconut or almond milk are really nice too)

- chopped fresh fruit e.g. strawberries, bananas, kiwi, blueberries, pears, grated apple

- a few coconut chips (optional)

- a dollop of yogam (2/3rds greek yoghurt mixed with 1/3rd thick cream)

- a drizzle of maple syrup

How to Prepare

~ Just mix your granola, fruit and coconut chips in a bowl and cover with milk

~ Top with the Yogam and maple syrup

Make~Life~Easier Tip: If you make some Fruit Sticks for dessert on the BBQ for supper, make a little extra and add this to your granola the next day. Oh my! You can also use some of the granola for the base of your Fruit Yogam dessert if you don't have any biscuits or fancy something healthier.

The Muffins

You're probably not going to make your own breakfast muffins but the shop-bought ones are pretty good with some nice toppings. We prefer the muffins pan-toasted (you can just dry-fry them on both sides in a frying pan) but you can eat them straight out of the packet too.

The general thinking on healthy eating is that it is good to have some protein at breakfast as this helps keep you satisfied until lunchtime and away from the biscuit tin. It's also good for campervan life as we often go off and do an active day after breakfast (hiking, cycling, surfing) and it helps to eat something substantial for breakfast.

The Toppings

- Crème cheese and roasted peppers (from shop-bought jar)

- Crème cheese and smoked salmon

- Crème cheese topped with strawberry slices

- Ranch beans (see recipe 'The Beans')

- Egg Mayog: chopped hard-boiled eggs mixed with Mayog i.e. half mayonnaise-half Greek yogurt (see recipe 'The Mayog')

- Mashed banana and a pinch of cinnamon

- Leftover Chilli con Beanie (see recipe 'The Chilli')

- Tuna Mayog: tin of tuna mixed with Mayog

- Nutella topped with slices of banana

- Peanut butter and marmalade

- Flat cheese (e.g. Edam, Gouda, Maasdam) on top of a thin layer of ginger jam. (Sounds weird but it really works!)

Lunches & Suppers

The Chilli

This is a recipe I adapted from the traditional Chilli con Carne ('Chilli with Meat') when I spent a few years as a vegetarian. It is so delicious and popular with my friends that I still cook it now that I am an omnivore again.

If you want to make the meaty version you can replace the tin of mixed beans with mince but you will need to brown the meat first and drain off the fat. Some of the tastiest and most nutritious meats to use for a chilli are venison and bison mince. We get our bison mince from Bush Farm Bison Centre near Warminster in Wiltshire. See: http://www.bisonfarm.co.uk. You can also camp at the centre and walk around the farm to see the happy bison grazing!

Ingredients (serves 4)

- oil for frying (2 tbsps)
- 1 large green pepper (chopped in to small pieces)
- 1 medium onion (chopped in to small pieces)
- i can of plum tomatoes (400g)
- 1 packet of chilli con carne spice mix
- 1 can kidney beans (400g)
- 1 can mixed beans (400g) or any other beans that you like: haricot, black~eyed etc.)

~ Heat the oil in a large saucepan and add the chopped pepper. Fry for 2~3 minutes.

~ Add the chopped onion and fry until both are soft.

~ Add the tin of plum tomatoes. Cook a little and break them up until the mixture is smooth.

~ Add the Chilli spice mix, stir and add some water if it is too thick.

~ Let this mixture cook gently for 5 minutes.

~ Add the drained can of kidney beans and the drained can of mixed beans. (If you are doing the meaty version, you can add the browned mince at this stage to replace the can of mixed beans.)

~ Let this cook gently for around 10 minutes, stirring occasionally so that it doesn't stick to the bottom.

Serve with a dollop of natural yogurt and a sprinkling of grated mature cheddar. You can eat it by itself or with rice and it's also nice on toast or on a baked potato (if you are cooking it at home). It also tastes good the following day and freezes well.

Chilli con Beanie

Make~Life~Easier Tip: *It's also great the next day in a quesadilla with some grated Cheddar cheese (see recipe for 'The Quesadilla').*

Nutrition Tip: *Beans may be an inexpensive, humble food but they are packed with goodness. They are a great source of healthy protein and fibre. They are also full of anti~oxidants and provide important vitamins and minerals including B vitamins, iron, folic acid, zinc and potassium.*

The Quesadilla

Quesadillas are made from tortillas which are cheap, easy to store and are amazingly versatile. You can fill the tortillas with virtually anything but you do really need to have some cheese in there somewhere ('queso' is 'cheese' in Spanish) as this melts and makes it nice and moist.

Ingredients

- a packet of soft tortillas (if you are gluten~intolerant you could try some corn tortillas)

- a cheese~based filling:

    o Cooked bacon pieces/grated cheddar/Fruit chutney/rocket

    o Crumbled Feta/grilled peppers in oil (buy these in a jar or at deli counter in supermarket)/rocket/black pepper

    o Grated cheddar/ tomato salsa (from jar)

    o Left~over chilli con Beanie/grated cheddar

    o Cooked chicken breast/grated cheddar/ pesto sauce (from jar or fresh)

    o Tuna from can/grated cheddar/rocket

~ Add a little light oil to a frying pan

~ Place your tortilla in the pan on a medium heat

~ Put your filling on half of the tortilla and fold the other half on top

~ Press down with a fish slice and cook for about a minute

~ Flip over and cook the other side for around 2 minutes

~ Remove from pan and cut in half to serve

Quesadillas filled with leftover Chilli con Beanie and cheddar cheese plus rocket salad

Make~Life~Easier Tip: Rocket is one of the best packet salads to have while you our out camping as, not only does it have a lovely peppery taste, if keeps better than most other salad leaves. To help any packet salad last a bit longer put a folded piece of kitchen roll in the bag as this soaks up the moisture and stops the leaves from going slimy.

The Risotto

Many people seem to be a little scared of risottos because they think that they are difficult but they really are not. Trust me. And the great thing about them is that they can be done in one frying pan and are a good way to use up any veg and other bits and pieces you have lying around.

A good risotto has a creamy feel to it and you mostly achieve this by adding the liquid stock in small amounts and letting it absorb in to the rice before adding the next amount. If you can't be fussed with that, you can add all the stock at the beginning although the rice will not be so nice and creamy (what I call 'smurgy'). However, I have added a twist to this recipe which guarantees a 'smurgy' risotto; a couple of dollops of cream cheese at the end!

Cheesy Chicken Risotto

Ingredients (serves 4)

- 3 tbsps light oil (preferably olive oil for flavour)
- 150g risotto (arborio) rice (around 7 heaped tbsps.)
- 1 red pepper chopped in to small pieces (about 1")
- 1 medium onion chopped in to small pieces (about 1")
- 6 or 7 small mushrooms (sliced)
- 2 chicken breasts cut in to bite-sized pieces
- ½ chicken stock cube (if you don't have this you

could use a tblsp. Of soy sauce or BBQ sauce)

• 2 heaped tbsps crème fraiche or cream cheese

•any herbs you fancy e.g. rosemary, oregano, basil, parsley (optional)

How to Cook

~ Add the oil to a large frying pan on a medium heat

~ Add the chopped vegetables and chicken pieces and fry for around 5 minutes

~ Add the dry rice to the pan and cook for a few minutes while stirring to make sure all the rice gets coated

~ Add 1 pint of hot water to half a chicken stock cube (or soy sauce/BBQ sauce) and pour 1/3rd of the hot stock in to the pan and stir. Cook gently until most of it has been absorbed.

~ Add the next 1/3rd of the stock and do the same

~ Add the final 1/3rd of the stock AND 2 tbsps. crème fraiche or crème cheese and stir

~ Add the herbs

~ Let the risotto cook until the stock has been absorbed and the rice is soft

Variations:

You can use **cooked prawns** or **smoked salmon** instead of the chicken but add these at the end and just give them a minute or two to warm through. You can also do the same with any leftover '10:10 Chicken' you may have cooked previously (see 'Small-Things-That-Make-a Big-Difference' section) or add both the fish and chicken and have a paella!

For vegetarians (or just because it's gorgeous), swop the red pepper for pieces of **cooked beetroot** and swop the chicken for **goat's cheese** or **feta cheese** but add these when you add the final 1/3rd of stock. You can also throw in some rocket or spinach for good measure.

Beetroot and Cheese Risotto

The Pan-Fry

This is a really quick way to healthily fry up some meat (or shellfish) with interesting spices and a few veg. It's great served with a grain side-dish like couscous, rice, or buckwheat (see 'The Side-Dish'), or in a wrap or pitta bread pocket for a light meal. It works best with chicken breast but you can also use steak or lamb. Large prawns are great too but you will need to cook these for less time.

Nowadays there are so many gorgeous spice mixes available in the big supermarkets and you can almost have a tour around the world by looking at the spice shelves. The combos I like best for this dish are:

~ Ras al Hanout (North Africa)

~ Garam Masala (India)

~ Jerk (Jamaica)

~ 5-Spice (China)

When you look at the ingredients of these spices you realise that they are not just tasty, they are medicine in a jar. As Pym, my teacher on a Thai cooking course said – "I am not only your chef, I am also your herbalist!"

Ingredients

- 2 x chicken breasts cut in to roughly 1" pieces

- 1 x medium onion cut in to 1" strips

- other chopped veg of your choice e.g. peppers, mushrooms

- 2 tbsps light oil

- 1 tsp spice mix (see above)

- 4 tbsps of fruit juice like: pomegranate, orange, pineapple or mango

How to Cook

~ Heat the oil in a frying pan over a medium heat

~ Add the onion and other chopped veg to the pan and fry until soft

~ Add the spice and fry for another 2 minutes while stirring

~ Add the meat pieces, the juice/honey and fry for another 10 minutes or until the meat is cooked through

Make~Life~Easier Tip: If you would like it a little sweeter you can add some maple syrup or honey to the fruit juice before you put it in the pan. If you make extra you can also use this as a dressing for your grain side-dish.

Every now and then a piece of kitchen kit comes along that makes you wonder how you ever lived without it. Silcone lids are one of those pieces of kit...

In case you haven't already come across the silicone phenomenon in the cookware world let me tell you a little about it. There are now many items of kitchen utensils and gadgetry that are made of gorgeous, colourful silicone. When you look at it, it looks like a piece of rubber that would melt if it went anywhere near heat but this material is actually incredibly heat resistant (up to 250 degrees centigrade) so can even go in the oven. You can actually buy muffin cases and bread 'tins' made of silicone but one of my favourite bits of silicone cookware is the silicone lids.

There are 2 types of lids:

1. The stiffer, flat ones that you use more as saucepan lids.

2. The 'floppy' ones with tabs that you stretch across a bowl/tin and you tend to use these for fridge storage or for covering food when you are eating outside.

The saucepan lids create quite a tight seal which means that your pan will boil a lot easier in windy conditions and you'll need to use less gas. They are really helpful in recipes like my '10-10 Chicken' that needs a tight lid on the pan while it is cooking and resting.

Both types of lids are really light, easy to store and virtually indestructible so great for the van.

You can buy them individually or in sets (6", 8" 10" etc.) and you can even get a small one to put on top of you mug of tea that helps to keep it warm and keep the insects out. My sister, who is a professional gardener, uses these all the time on her mugs of tea when she is working outside.

If you are going to be on hook~up most of the time a portable induction hob is invaluable. You can buy the single~ring ones on Amazon/eBay starting around £30 and they are really worth it as, if you are paying for hook~up, you might as well use the electric instead of your gas.

They are easy to use and are very safe as there is no flame and the only area of the cooker that gets heated is under the pan. You will need to have pans/kettle with a stainless steel bottom as aluminium ones do not work but the Collaps Kettle from Outwell does have a stainless steel bottom and it boils the water in no time.

The Salad

SALAD 1: Girona Salad

This dish is based on a salad that Glyn and I had at a restaurant while we were in Girona in Spain, hence the name. It brings back a wonderful memory of sitting outside in the square by the cathedral watching the world go by and listening to a street musician playing haunting music on a hang drum (Search **'hang drum'** on YouTube and enjoy!)

Ingredients (Serves 2)

- 6 or 7 robust lettuce leaves e.g. romaine or cos

- 2 cooked chicken breasts. You can buy these ready~cooked from the supermarket or cut the raw breasts of chicken in to bite-size pieces and pan-fry. You can also use any chicken you have may left from cooking chicken breasts using the 10-10 method (see '10-10 chicken' recipe)

- a ripe pear

- a handful of walnut pieces

- 100g-ish of blue cheese e.g. danish blue, stilton

- a drizzle of a honey & mustard dressing

How to Make

~ Tear the lettuce and put in a large bowl.

~ Add the chicken breast pieces to the lettuce.

~ Cut the ripe pear in to small chunks and add to the lettuce

~ Pour over the salad dressing and toss to coat all ingredients

~ Crumble the cheese and add to the salad

~ Toss the walnut pieces in to the salad

This makes a lovely light meal in itself but if you need to make it a bit more filling serve with some crusty bread and butter.

Make~Life~Easier Tip : You can leave out the chicken and just make it as a tasty side-salad to your barbequed or pan-fried meat and fish. To pep up your side salads here are some unusual ingredients that you might not have thought about that you can add:

o ripe strawberry pieces

o dried coconut shavings

o fresh peas (uncooked)

o blackcurrants (lovely micro-bursts of flavour)

o flaked almonds

SALAD 2: Micro Salad

Sometimes it's nice to have a salad that's really fresh and crunchy and a micro salad is also a great way to use up any small amounts of raw veg that you have lying around. The dressing is what makes it special and you can use any or your favourite ones that you buy in a bottle or, for the best results, make up your own (see 'Honey & Mustard Dressing' and 'Raspberry Vinaigrette' from the 'Small Things that Make a Big Difference' section).

Rainbow Micro Salad

Basically you just chop up lots of different raw veg in to pieces that are no more than ½" long and dress with a salad dressing. The sort of veg that work well for this are:

- red onions
- red cabbage
- courgettes
- celery
- carrot
- red pepper
- mange tout
- broccoli
- cauliflower
- radish

You can also add fruit, like apples, pears, raspberries, or nuts such as walnuts, cashews, almonds.

Rainbow Micro Salad with Raspberry Vinaigrette

Nutrition Tip: *When we Eat-the-Rainbow we are giving ourselves some amazing nutrition as each colour represents a different, health-giving nutrient. For example, orange, red and yellow foods give us zeaxanthin, flavonoids, lycopene, potassium, vitamin C and beta~carotene, which is vitamin A. Green vegetables are sources of vitamin K, folic acid, potassium, as well as carotenoids and omega-3 fatty acids. Purple/blue foods get their bright colour from anthocyanins, which have been linked with antioxidants and anti-aging properties in the body.*

69

Deki's Greek Salad

This is a really easy salad recipe from Deki Dakar, co~owner of The Magic Café in Oxford. The café has a laid-back, alternative vibe and serves home-cooked vegetarian food including some healthy, robust salads of which this is one. As I don't eat tomatoes or cucumber I can't tell you what this one tastes like but it is really popular in the café.

Ingredients (Serves 2~4)

The Salad

- 3 fresh tomatoes chopped in to bite-size pieces
- half a cucumber chopped in to bite-size pieces
- 1 medium red onion chopped in to 1 inch strands
- 8-10 black olives
- 1 packet of feta cheese cut in to small cubes

The Dressing

- 3 tbsp olive oil
- 1 tsp dried oregano
- pinch of salt
- pinch of pepper

To Prepare

~ Put all the salad ingredients in a bowl

~ Mix all the dressing ingredients together and pour over the salad

And that's it!

Make~Life~Easier Tip: *Sometimes you can buy the Feta cheese already cut in to cubes and it is normally in a tub in the cheese chill cabinet.*

These ingredients can also be used in these other recipes so it's worth buying a bit extra. Use in: quesadillas, toasted sandwiches, wraps, side dishes, risotto, pasta, muffin toppings, frittatas. Just get creative and experiment!

The Soup 'n' Sarnie

This is a really nice combo that works well as a lunch or light supper. We prefer to have our sandwiches toasted and we have invested in a small electric sandwich maker but, naturally, you would need to be on hook-up to use this. However, you can toast your sandwiches in a dry frying pan too.

I love making fresh soups at home but, personally, I find it too much of faff to do when we are out camping and you really need an electric blender which we just wouldn't carry in the van. So we just buy a pot one of the fresh soups from the chill cabinet in the supermarket and these are pretty good anyway so there seems no point in re-inventing the wheel.

Here are some of the sandwiches fillings that we like:

• Cooked chicken pieces (pan-fry chicken or just use some 10-10 Chicken) with a dollop of Sweet Chilli Mayog Sauce (add a dollop of sweet chilli sauce from a bottle to a dollop of Mayog i.e half Greek yogurt, half mayonnaise) and some rocket leaves

• Cooked prawns with Sweet Chilli Mayog and rocket

• Blue cheese and mango chutney (or any other fruit chutney)

• Grated cheddar cheese and Branston pickle

• Tuna Mayog and grated cheddar cheese

- Hummus, cheddar cheese & tomato

Eat your sarnie with a hot bowl of soup. We like these ones but go with whatever floats your boat:

- Mushroom Soup

- Sweet Potato, Coconut and Chilli

- Carrot Soup

- Spicy Parsnip Soup

- Spicy Lentil

- Tomato and Basil

How to Cook

If you are using a sandwich maker then just follow the instructions but to pan-fry your toastie just fill your sandwich and put it in a dry frying pan on medium heat. Press down with a fish slice for a couple of minutes until the bottom bread is nice and brown. Flip over carefully and do the same on the other side for a couple of minutes until the sandwich feels like it has melted inside.

The Pasta

This is an incredibly easy, one-pot pasta recipe that is great hot or cold. We love to cook this on a beach in the evening while we watch the sun go down with a glass of red wine. Yay!

One-Pot Pasta Genovese

Ingredients (Serves 3-4)

- small, new potatoes (skin on) chopped into quarters (half a kilo which is roughly half a bag)

- fine green beans chopped into 1" pieces (150g which is about half a bag)

- dried pasta such as fusilli or penne (200g which is about a third of a bag)

- 1 pot of fresh green pesto (150g) or around 3 tablespoons of pesto from a jar

How to Cook

~ Heat around 1.5 litres of water in a large saucepan until boiling.

~ Add the chopped potatoes to the water and cook for 10 minutes.

~ Add the chopped green beans and the pasta to the water and let it cook for another 10 minutes.

~ Drain the water off.

~ Add the pesto to the saucepan and mix with the potatoes, beans and pasta until all are well coated and serve

This dish is great served with crusty bread or a green salad.

One-Pot Pasta Genovese

Make~Life~Easier Tip: If you have any leftovers they keep well in the fridge and make a nice cold pasta accompaniment for barbequed meat or fish the next day.

'Tuna Chuck-up'

This recipe was donated by my Aussie friend, Penny Bassett, and her husband Tim who have been camping around the world for many years and now own a Nissan NV 200 campervan (converted by Sussex Campervans) called Nissy.

The dish was named by Penny's son when he went to university and it became one of his favourite quick and easy meals. They have now adapted it for their campervan life and would like to share it with you.

Ingredients (Enough for 2 hungry people)

- 2 mugs pasta (approx 200 grams)
- 160 gm can of tuna in oil
- 1 large onion, coarsely chopped
- ½ red pepper, chopped chunky
- 1 clove garlic, chopped fine
- fresh or dried chilli (optional)
- 3 or 4 medium tomatoes, quartered
- salt and pepper
- grated cheese to add when served

~ Cook pasta in salted boiling water for approximately 10 minutes and then drain.

~ While the pasta is cooking, pour the oil from the tuna, reserving a couple of tablespoons and use this to fry the onion and pepper.

~ When the onions and pepper are softened, add the tomatoes and cook for about five minutes till the tomatoes are a bit squidgy, or less if you prefer them firm.

~ Add the garlic and the drained tuna, keeping it chunky. Heat through for a few minutes being careful not to break the tuna up too much (just because it looks nicer!)

~ Season with salt and pepper and chilli if you like it.

~ Mix with the pasta and serve in bowls, sprinkled with grated cheese.

There are many variations on this recipe ~ olives, sweetcorn, mushrooms, capers, chopped gherkins all go well with this meal and a couple of spoonfuls of cream just before mixing make it even tastier.

Thanks, Pen & Tim!

The Kebab

If you have a barbeque, even if it's just a disposable one, then kebabs make a nice change to the usual burgers and bangers. They are great served with a grain side-dish or just with a fresh, green salad. I offer you a couple of meaty versions and a veggie version.

P.S. Barbequed pineapple is outrageously gorgeous (and, surprisingly, so is barbecued water melon)!

KEBAB 1: Saucy Chicken Kebab

Ingredients (serves 2)

- 2 x chicken breasts cut in to roughly 1" pieces

- 1 packet of pineapple chunks (you can buy these already cut in the fruit chill cabinet)

- 3 tbsps soy sauce

- 2 tablespoons marmalade

- 1 tbsps light oil

How to Cook

~ Mix the soy sauce, marmalade and oil in a bowl

~ Add the chicken pieces to the bowl and let it marinate in the fridge for at least half an hour

~ Thread the chicken pieces on to a kebab skewer, alternating with pineapple chunks

~ Cook the kebab on the barbeque turning occasionally and basting with the remaining dressing until the meat is cooked through

KEBAB 2: Cheeky Cheese Kebab

Ingredients (serves 2)

• 1 x 226g packet of paneer cheese (indian cheese) cut in to 1" cubes approx

• sweet chilli dipping sauce

How to Cook

~ Put 2-3 tbsps sweet chilli sauce in a bowl

~ Add the paneer pieces to the bowl, mix to coat and let it marinate for at least 20 minutes

~ Thread the cheese pieces on to kebab skewers

~ Cook the kebab on the barbeque turning occasionally until the cheese has a nice, charred look to it

~ Serve and dip in the remaining sweet chilli sauce

KEBAB 3: Mouth-watering Meatball Kebab

Ingredients (serves 2)

- 1 x 450g pack of pre-made meatballs
- 10-ish cherry tomatoes
- a medium courgette cut in to 1" sections

How to Cook

~ Thread the meatballs on to a kebab skewer alternating with the cherry tomatoes and courgette pieces

~ Cook the kebab on the barbeque turning occasionally until the meatballs are cooked and the veg has a nice, charred look to it

~ Serve and dip in any of the BBQ sauces (see 'BBQ Sauces') that take your fancy

Mouth-watering Meatball Kebab

Paneer cheese kebabs marinated in Sweet Chill dipping sauce

Saucy Chicken and Pineapple Kebabs on a Hubcap

This is a clever pan that can turn your gas ring in to a grill/BBQ. It really does look like a hubcap which has a bottom pan and a domed section on top where you put the food for cooking. A little 'moat' on the bottom pan collects any fat/juices and also keeps the food warm with steam. Great for flash grilling a couple of steaks or for mini kebabs. They cost around £10 and you can get them from Bright Spark or Amazon.

The Eggs

Catalan Eggs

This is a lovely, light but filling meal for a warm summer's day. I learned it many years ago when I worked on a charter yacht in Barcelona in Spain so I call it 'Catalan Eggs'.

Ingredients (Serves 2)

- 4 hard-boiled eggs (2 each)

- 2-3 tbsp mayog (half mayonnaise, half greek yoghurt mixed together)

- 2 x 160g cans of tuna (in brine or spring water - drained)

- jar of chargrilled red peppers (optional)

- packet of green salad leaves

- honey & mustard dressing from shop or homemade (see honey & mustard dressing in the Small Things That Make a Big Difference section)

How to Cook

~ Gently add the eggs to a pan of boiling water and cook for at least 6 minutes until the eggs are hard-boiled. Let the eggs cool completely.

~ While the eggs are boiling, drain the cans of tuna

and put the flakes in to a bowl. Add the Mayog to the tuna and mix.

~ Peel the eggs and cut in half lengthways and remove the yolks to a dish and crumble the yolks up in to small pieces

~ Add a large dollop of the tuna Mayog to the hole left in the egg whites by the yolks

~ Sprinkle some of the egg yolk on top of the tuna Mayog on the eggs.

~ Put a few, thin strips of the red peppers from the jar on top of the eggs

~ Dress the salad with the Honey & Mustard dressing and serve with the eggs

Catalan Eggs

Make~Life~Easier Tip: *If you have any Tuna Mayog leftover you can put it on a toasted muffin for breakfast next morning or add some sweet corn to it and have it in a sandwich or a wrap when you are out and about.*

The Side Dish

Sometimes it's nice to have something from the grain family as a side dish and the easy-cook grains that work well for campervan cooking are:

- Rice

- Couscous

- Buckwheat

- Bulgar wheat

Please don't be put off if these are things you've never heard of before because they are all now readily available in supermarkets and they are so easy to cook. Also, they come dried in a packet so keep for a long time and are easy to store. You can add so many different, tasty 'bits' to them once you have cooked the grain and you can dress them with lovely healthy dressings. They are great hot or cold so you can keep the leftovers in the fridge for the next day to have with your BBQ'd meat or fish.

N.B If you are gluten-intolerant please bear in mind that couscous and bulgar wheat are made from wheat

Ingredients

So what sort of 'bits' can you add?

- **nuts**: flaked almonds, walnuts, cashews, hazelnuts, pine nuts. (these all taste better if you gently dry, pan-fry them first to get them a bit toasted but it's not essential. Also you can do this at home before you go.)

- **veg**: peas, broccoli, green beans, bell peppers, courgettes, sun-dried tomatoes, spring onions.

- **beans/peas**: kidney beans, chickpeas, broad beans from a tin

- **fruit**: pineapple, apple, pear, strawberries, coconut chips, blackcurrants, sultanas

- **herbs**: mint, dill, coriander, parsley

- **spices**: cumin, fivespice, ras al hanout, jerk, garam masala, ground or grated ginger, chilli (add the chilli or ginger to an oil or other liquid before dressing)

Dressings

You can use things like: lemon juice, olive oil, soy sauce, fruit juices mixed with maple syrup (pomegranate juice works really well), coconut milk, Honey & Mustard Dressing (see 'Small Things That Make a Big Difference'), or any bottled dressing that you love. You can also add around half a tsp of your spice of choice to the dressing to pep it up.

How to Cook

~ First you need to cook your grain according to the instructions on the packet. (Couscous doesn't need to be cooked on the stove, you just pour boiling water on it and let it stand covered for a few minutes)

~ Add your 'bits'

~ Dress with the dressing

Here are some of the Combos that we Like:

Classy Couscous

Cook the couscous according to the instructions on the packet.

Add: toasted flaked almonds/sultanas/ I tbsp. chopped mint

Dressing: 3-4 tbsp pomegranate juice/ 1 tbsp maple syrup/ 1/2 tsp Ras al Hanout spice

Tip: soak the sultanas in a little warm water for about 10 minutes before adding to the dish and use the sweet water in the dressing.

Dreamy Creamy Rice

Cook the rice according to the instructions on the packet

Add: chickpeas from a tin/toasted flaked almonds/ 1 tbsp chopped coriander

Dressing: half coconut milk (from a tin)/half water

Garden Buckwheat

Pour some boiling water on to some roasted buckwheat (roughly twice the amount of water as buckwheat). Let it steep for 5 minutes and pour off the liquid (this can be drunk as a delicious, nourishing tea).

Add: micro-broccoli florets/broad beans from a tin/1 tbsp chopped mint

Dressing: half olive oil, half lemon juice

N.B. If you prefer, you can use Bulgar wheat in place of any of the grains above. Just cook according to the packet.

You get the idea! Try out different combos for yourself. Sometimes I have discovered a really nice combo simply by combining what I had available.

The Curry

A curry is a great meal for when you are out in the campervan as you can normally make it in one pan. Making the curry from scratch with freshly~cooked spices gives the best results but there are now so many good 'curry kits' in the supermarkets that it is much easier to use these when you are out having adventures. They are small and easy to store and it means that you don't have to carry a lot of different ingredients. Of course, you'll need to buy the fresh ingredients such as the meat and veg.

Here are a couple of my favourite curry~kit recipes:

CURRY 1: Korma Curry (The Spice Tailor)

Ingredients (serves 2)

- one Spice Tailor Delicate Korma curry kit
- 2 chicken breasts, diced
- 5-6 mushrooms, sliced
- 1 tbsp light oil

How to Cook

~ Heat the oil in a saucepan and cook the dry spices (provided) for around 30 seconds

~ Add the chicken, mushrooms and base sauce (provided) and cook for 2-3 minutes

~ Add the main sauce (provided) and a splash of water and simmer until the chicken is cooked (about 5 minutes)

~ Serve with rice or naan bread

CURRY 2: Easy Thai Green Curry (Thai Taste)

Ingredients (Serves 2)

- 1 x Easy Thai Green Curry Kit from Thai Taste

- 2 chicken breasts, diced

- 1 tbsp of light oil

- 100g green beans (chopped in to 1" pieces)

- 1 small carrot (sliced in to diagonal, thin rounds)

How to Cook

~ Heat the oil to a saucepan and add the curry paste (provided) and 1 tbsp of the coconut milk (provided) and fry for around 3 minutes

~ Add the chicken and fry for a further 3 minutes

~ Add the rest of the coconut milk and the carrot and green beans and cook for another 5-10 minutes or until the chicken is cooked through

~ Add the sachet of herbs (provided) and simmer for 3 minutes

~ Serve with rice

Both of these curries would also work well using large prawns or just vegetables instead of the chicken. The Korma also works well with Paneer cheese cut in to cubes.

Make~Life~Easier~Tip: *If you have any leftover curry (really?), you could mix it with some cooked rice to have as a side dish for your BBQ the next day.*

The BBQ Sauce

BBQs are great for outdoor cooking and they can range from the humble disposable silver-tray ones up to gorgeous fancy pieces of kit like the Cadac Safari Chef.

Campers mostly cook burgers and bangers (that's sausages for the non~Brits) which are great and you can find some really good butcher-made ones at local farmers and village markets so you're probably not going to making your own. But I would encourage you to get a little more adventurous and try some Kebabs (see 'The Kebab') and also remember that fish is pretty amazing BBQ'd as well (BBQ'd salmon steak is to die for).

However, in Camper Cookie land we always like to make things just a little tastier so I offer you some sauces to dollop on whatever meat or fish you are BBQ-ing and you can mix-and-match to whatever works for your taste-buds.

SAUCE 1: Mayog Sauces

Mayog is a mixture of mayonnaise and Greek yoghurt (roughly half and half) and you can add lots of readymade sauces to this depending on what you have and what you fancy such as:

- sweet chilli dipping sauce

- mango chutney

- any fruit chutney that you find on your travels

• Barbecue Honey Sauce (bought)

I usually find that half Mayog to half sauce is about right.

SAUCE 2: Cheat's Satay Sauce

Just mix together:

- 2 tbsp peanut butter

- 2 tbsp soy sauce

- 2 tbsp sweet chilli sauce

This is great with both meat and fish.

However, if you want to make a really zingy, healthy sauce for the BBQ try Geeta's Ketchup and Mint Chutney...

Here is a really fresh and easy chutney to have with your BBQ'd meat and fish. It's from Geeta at the Delish Cookery School in Bristol at www.delishcook.co.uk.

Ketchup and Mint Chutney

Ingredients (Serves 2-4)

- Tomato ketchup

- 2 tsp mint sauce

- 1 carrot

- white or red onion

- 1 tsp garam masala

- crushed green chillies (optional)

- handful coriander

Preparation

~ In a mixing bowl squirt a good glug of tomato ketchup. Add 2 tsp of mint sauce and mix thoroughly

~ Add a little water until thin consistency

~ Using an electric chopper (if you are at home) or a sharp knife, dice the carrot and onion, until small. Do not blend to a puree. Add this to the ketchup mixture and stir

~ Now season, using 1 tsp Garam Masala, salt and crushed green chillies (optional to taste)

~ To finish add finely chopped coriander

~ Taste and adjust seasoning.

Desserts

The Fruit Stick

A lot of the time, **it is summer when we are out having adventures** in our campervan which is when fruit is at its best so it would be rude not to make the most of it. One of the best ways to enjoy fruit is to make a Fruit Stick, basically a fruit kebab, which you cook on the BBQ or on your Hubcap grill (see 'Kit Tip: The Hubcap' or search it on YouTube). When you cook fruit in this way it caramelises and becomes gorgeously sweet and juicy.

Here is one of my favourite combos:

Fruit-Stick from Heaven

Ingredients (suggest 2 sticks per person)

- some fresh pineapple cut in to 1" cubes (or just buy some ready-cut cubes from the fruit chill cabinet)
- some large-ish strawberries
- some ripe peaches or nectarines cut in to 1" pieces
- 2 tbsps of maple syrup mixed with a tsp of light oil

How to Cook

- Thread the fruit pieces on to a metal kebab stick or pre-soaked wooden ones

- Brush the fruit with a light coating of maple syrup

- Cook on the BBQ (or Hubcap) for around 10 minutes, turning occasionally, until the fruit looks slightly browned

- Remove from the stick and enjoy or take it to the next level (see below)

Fruit-Stick Lush

Serve the cooked fruit with a dollop or two of Yogam (2/3rds Greek yoghurt mixed with 1/3rd thick cream)

Fruit Stick Fondue

Dip the cooked fruit in a thick chocolate sauce. An easy way to make the chocolate sauce is to just drop some chocolate chunks in to a small saucepan with a little cream and heat very gently while stirring until the chocolate has melted and combined to make a thick sauce.

Make Life Easier Tip: Gu make a thick and gorgeous, pre-made hot chocolate which you can buy in cartons (Sainsburys and Waitrose) and you could just heat this up for your chocolate fondue. You can also have any that is left (not on my watch!) to make a dreamy hot (or cold) chocolate drink. It says to heat in the microwave but I find it heats just as well in a saucepan and I like to thin it a little with coconut milk. It also comes in Salted Caramel and Mocha flavours (swoon).

The Banana

Bananas are a really useful thing to have in a camping larder. Not only are they a neatly-wrapped, high-energy snack to take out with you, they can be used in so many different ways. I love them mashed with a little cinnamon on a muffin in the morning but they are at their best in desserts. Here are a couple of quite naughty desserts that both adults and kids will love.

BANANAS 1: Bananas-and-Custard with a Twist

Ingredients (serves 2)

- 2 bananas

- 1 packet of instant custard that you make with just boiling water

- 1 Mars Bar

How to Make

~ Peel the bananas and chop in to bite-sized pieces

~ Chop the Mars Bar in to small pieces

~ Make up the custard according to the instructions on the packet

~ Place the banana pieces and Mars Bar bits in a large

bowl and pour the custard over them

~ Allow the custard to cool a little and serve

The hot custard will slightly melt the Mars Bar which is really good. If you want to make the recipe a little healthier you could use dark chocolate instead of the Mars Bar.

If you want to be extra naughty, replace the Mars Bar with some chopped-up Chocolate Cupcakes – the kids will love it (ok, and the adults too!)

BANANAS 2: BBQ Banana

Ingredients (serves 2)

- 2 bananas

- 1 Mars Bar

- a couple of teaspoons of yogam (third thick cream, two~thirds greek yoghurt)

How to Make it

~ Leaving the banana in its skin, cut a large groove down the middle

~ Chop the Mars Bar in to small pieces and stuff it in to the groove in the banana

~ Wrap in foil and place on the BBQ for 10-15 minutes depending on how hot your barbeque is

~ When it's all melty, remove it from the foil and put each cooked banana in a dish and serve with a dollop of Yogam

Magical Moment

This dish always brings back fond memories for me as it was made by our guide when we were on a camping safari in Namibia many years ago. We were cooking up supper over an open fire on the Skeleton coast which is one of the most surreal landscapes I have ever been in. Isn't our planet amazing!

The Fruit-Yogam

The Naughty Fruit-Yogam

Sometimes, at the end of the day, you just need a naughty dessert and my Fruit-Yogam is just that, except that it is not as naughty as it feels so you can enjoy it without guilt.

Once you get the idea of the basic blueprint, you can start adding all sorts of things to it. Glyn often makes himself a super-deluxe version at home which has virtually everything in it; every fruit in the house, several types of yoghurt and biscuits galore (often with meringue as well!). Sometimes, I think, less is more but go with whatever floats your boat.

Ingredients (Serves 2)

- 4 x crushed biscuits (Glyn and I like Oreos, shortbread, ginger ones or try some meringue)

- 4 tbsps greek yoghurt

- 2 tbsps thick cream

- 3 slices of tinned mango chopped in to small pieces

- 2 – 4 squares of dark chocolate, grated or chopped

- passionfruit & mango coulis (fruit puree) from a bottle (optional but gorgeous)

How to Prepare

~ Create the Yogam by mixing the yoghurt and cream together in a bowl

~ Add the mango pieces to the Yogam and mix through

~ Divide the crushed biscuits in half and put in to the bottom of two drinking glasses

~ Spoon half the mango Yogam on top

~ Swirl the coulis on top of the Yogam

~ Put the rest of the mango Yogam on top of the coulis

~ Sprinkle the chopped dark chocolate on top

This dessert also works well with fresh raspberries instead of the tinned mango and using a raspberry coulis instead of the passionfruit & mango one. Of course, this dessert is yummy even without the coulis but it does make it extra special. There are lots of different ready-made fruit coulis in the supermarkets now for around £2 a bottle so go and have fun. You will wonder how you ever lived without them!

Guest Recipe:

My Fruit-Yogam Recipe was inspired by Fionna Page who is a registered Dietician so she is keen to make good, healthy food for her son Cormac (aged 6) but try and keep it fun too. This is their simpler dessert that Cormac calls his Fruit-Yoghurt Surprise. The ingredients are all just put in to one glass!

Ingredients (serves 1 glass per person)

• chopped fruit such as: strawberries, kiwi, blueberries, banana or any combo. Tinned fruit can be used too (peaches are particularly good)

• yoghurt (natural or flavoured)

• crumbled biscuit of choice

To Prepare

~ Put your biscuit of choice in a freezer bag and bash with the bottom of a sturdy mug until it is in crumbs (you could use your mallet but take care not to destroy the biscuit completely!)

~ Place your chopped fruit in the base of a glass or tumbler

~ Spoon the yogurt on top

~ Sprinkle some of the biscuit crumbs on top

And that's it!

Fruit Yogam

Make~Life~Easier Tip: *You can also use the leftover tinned mango chopped in to one of the grain side dishes (goes well with rice) and use some of the juice with a spice added to dress the cooked grain (See 'The Side Dish').*

Drinks

The Soda

On a hot summer's day it is nice to have a fizzy drink that is really refreshing so here are two of the most refreshing drinks I know (and they are healthy too!).

Lime Zinger

Ingredients (serves 2)

- 2 fresh limes

- 1 large bottle of sparkling water (the colder the better)

How to Make

~ Squeeze the juice from the limes (if you don't have a squeezer just use your hands but roll the limes on a table top first to make sure that they are nice and juicy)

~ Take 2 glasses and put half the lime juice in to each one

~ Put 1 tsps of sugar (or xylitol*) in to each glass and stir to dissolve it in the lime juice

~ Pour the fizzy water on top to the strength you like it

Pineapple Quencher

Ingredients

- 1 carton of proper pineapple juice
- 1 medium bottle or can of lemonade

How to Make it

~ fill half a tall glass with pineapple juice

~ top up with the lemonade and stir to mix

Nutrition Tip: Limes are high in Vitamin C and pineapple contains an enzyme called bromelain which helps you digest protein.

*Xylitol is a healthy replacement for sugar and you can buy it in supermarkets on the sugar shelves.

Obviously it is impossible to go camping without having lots of cups of tea so having a kettle of some kind is important. The problem is, kettles are an awkward shape so are not so easy to store if you are tight on space.

However, Outwell have come up with the solution; their silicone **Collaps Kettle** is brilliant as it squashes down flat. It also seems pretty indestructible and, because the kettle has a stainless steel bottom, it will work on an induction hob as well as gas and, on the induction, it boils in just a minute or two. What's not to like!

The Cocktail

The Pommie Pleaser

No this is not what Australians call a cup of tea LoL! This is a gorgeous combo of fruit juices (and wine if you want to make it alcoh-frolic) that is just perfect for a summer evening.

Ingredients

- 1/3rd pomegranate juice (available in most supermarkets now)

- 1/3rd orange juice

- 1/3rd fizzy mixer (you can use: sparkling water, lemonade, sparkling wine or replace the orange juice and mixer with bucks fizz)

- a squeeze of fresh lime (optional)

How to Make

Just mix them all together in your glass or, if you are feeling posh, mix them in a glass jug and add a sprig or two of fresh mint. (*If you have any pomegranate and orange juice left over, just mix them together for a lovely breakfast juice the next day!*)

Pommie Pleaser Cocktail

Nutrition Tip: Pomegranates contain powerful anti-oxidants and are anti-inflammatory which means they help our bodies cope with the stresses that modern life puts us under. They also have Vitamin K which is good for bone health and maintaining healthy blood pressure.

The Chai Latte

Sometimes, in the evenings, you want something that is a bit warming but you haven't quite reached the hot chocolate craving level and a chai latte is a really satisfying option. Chai is spicy tea, usually made with lovely comforting spices like ginger, black pepper, cinnamon, fennel, cardamom and, if you make it with a milk base rather than just water, it becomes a latte.

Cheats Chai Latte

Ingredients (serves 1)

- ½ Mug of water
- ½ mug milk
- 1 masala chai teabag
- 1 tsp of sugar (or xylitol*)

How to Make

~ Put the water, milk, teabag and sugar in to a saucepan

~ Simmer gently for around 10 minutes

~ Remove the teabag and serve in a mug

Serious Chai Latte

Ingredients (serves 2)

- a mug of milk
- a mug of water
- 2 regular teabags (something light like Darjeeling is best)
- 1 level tsp of chai spice mix (see below)
- 1 tsp sugar (or xylitol*)

How to Make It

~ Put the water, milk, sugar, teabag and spice in to a saucepan

~ Simmer gently for around 10 minutes

~ Remove the teabag and serve in a mug

Chai Spice Mix

You can buy ready-made chai spice mix online but if you want to make your own and take it with you this is a nice combo:

- 1 tbsp black pepper
- 1 tbsp ground ginger
- 1 tbsp ground cinnamon
- 1 tbsp ground cardamom

• 1 tsp ground nutmeg

Just mix them all together and store in a small spice jar. You can adjust the amounts of each spice according to your personal taste.

Nutrition Tip: *Cinnamon is known to balance blood sugar, ginger is great for joints, fennel is good for digestion, black pepper is good for circulation and nutmeg is good for happiness. So as you can see, it's medicine in a jar!*

*Xylitol is a healthy replacement for sugar and you can buy it supermarkets on the sugar shelves

Kit Tip: Micro Pots

When you are out and about shopping look out for any useful micro pots and jars. These are great for taking away small amounts of sauce/coulis/pickles/spices etc . But make sure that they have a secure lid

The Hot Chocolate

Even in the summer, the evenings can be quite cool and it is nice to have a hot chocolate to sip while you sit beside the campervan and talk about life, the universe and everything. Of course there are packets of instant hot chocolate powders but, to me, these can sometimes taste a bit 'soapy'. So here are some easy ways to make really yummy hot choc and you can have fun experimenting to find your favourite version.

'I'm-Twelve-Again' Hot Choc

Ingredients (per person)

- A mugful of milk (coconut milk works really well too)

- your chocolate spread of choice e.g. Nutella, Reeses or any of the range of chocolate spreads that you can find in the supermarkets now. You can even buy some spreads that are based on well-known chocolate bars like Bounty, Maltesers or Cadburys caramel. If you prefer something a little more sophisticated, Waitrose do their own, high~quality dark chocolate spread.

How to Prepare

~ Heat the milk slowly in a saucepan

~ When it is hot but not boiling pour it in to a mug

~ Stir in 1-3 tsp of your chocolate spread of choice

And then just sit back and enjoy!

To make a slightly healthier version:

Ingredients (per person)

- a mugful of milk

- 4 chunks of a good-quality dark chocolate (broken-up or roughly chopped)

- 1/2 to 1 tsp of honey or xylitol (find it on the sugar aisle in supermarkets)

How to Prepare

~ Add the milk to a small saucepan and drop the chocolate in to the milk

~ Let it continue to heat gently while stirring until the chocolate melts

~ Before the milk reaches boiling point, add the honey or xylitol to taste and stir to dissolve

~ Serve in a mug

For the grown-ups, try adding a small slug of brandy to your hot choc – it's really warming and you'll sleep well. You can buy small bottles (35cl) of brandy in plastic bottles in the supermarkets now and these store easier than the glass ones.

Bake-Before-You-Go

The Trail Mix

Let's face it, you can't really have camping adventures without some trail mix. A trail mix is defined as – "a mixture of dried fruit and nuts eaten as a snack food, originally by walkers and campers" but here in Camper Cookie land it is so much more.

I regularly make up a batch of Trail Mix and keep it in a jar at home to have as a quick snack when I get the munchies mid-morning or late afternoon and Glyn sometimes takes some to work. If you keep a supply at home you can just throw some in to tupperware or a jar and take it with you when you are going off on a trip.

The Camper Cookie Trail Mix Blueprint

A Camper Cookie Trail Mix is made from a selection of:

- **nuts**: cashews, pecans, hazelnuts, walnuts, almonds, macadamia, brazils

- **seeds:** pumpkin seeds, sunflower seeds

- **dried** fruit: cranberries, apricots, blueberries, coconut chips, mango, banana, apple, sultanas

- **sweeties**: chocolate chips, chocolate raisins, yoghurt drops, micro fudge pieces, smarties

Basically you can combine any of the above but, to make it extra tasty, it is nice to roast the seeds and/or nuts first (roast in oven or fry in dry frying-pan). It's best to make the mix around 50% nuts, 20% seeds, 20% dried fruit and 10% sweeties but just do whatever feels good to you.

Here is one of our favourite combos:

Vanilla Trail Mix

Ingredients (makes a lot)

- 150g of pumpkin seeds
- 100g hazelnuts
- 200g cashew nuts
- 100g of dried cranberries
- 100g large sultanas
- 100g of chocolate chips

For the coating for the pumpkin seeds

- 2 tbsp coconut oil (you may need to gently melt this in the microwave first to get it runny)
- 1 tsp vanilla extract
- 3 tbsp runny honey

How to Prepare

~ Melt the coconut oil in a bowl and add the runny honey and vanilla extract

~ Toss the pumpkin seeds in the oil mixture and then lay them out evenly on a baking tray

~ Lay the nuts out on another dry baking tray

~ Preheat the oven to 160 degrees C

~ Put the nuts in the oven on the top shelf and the seeds on the middle shelf

~ Let them roast for around 15 minutes making sure that you stir them a couple of times so that they don't burn

~ When they are done take the nuts & seeds out of the oven and allow them to cool

~ Mix all ingredients together and store in a jar/tin/tupperware

Vanilla Trail Mix

Make~Life~Easier Tip: *If you have added chocolate chips or Smarties to your trail mix you might want to store it in the fridge as these melt in a hot campervan. However, when they cool off again they form some interesting clusters which I quite like.*

The Cookie

What would life be without a biscuit! And, for me, there is nothing quite as good as a cookie that you have made yourself – crispy on the outside and gooey on the inside. This does mean that you have to get the cooking time just right for your particular gooeyness factor which means that you'll have to bake (and eat) lots of cookies until you get it just right. Oh well, we must endure...

Comfort Cookies

Ingredients (makes about 12 cookies)

- 125g butter
- 200g soft brown sugar
- 1 egg (beaten)
- 1 tsp vanilla extract
- 200g self~raising flour
- ½ tsp of salt
- 200g chocolate chips

How to Make

~ Cream butter and sugar

~ Add the beaten egg and vanilla extract

~ Sift in the flour and add salt and chocolate chips

~ Make the dough in to golf~ball sized balls and put on to a baking tray lined with baking paper (leave plenty of space as they do spread)

~ Cook in a 175 degree C oven for around 7-10 minutes. Cooking less will mean that they have a gooier centre

~ Lift out carefully (as they are still soft) and let them cool on a baking tray

This is the recipe for the basic cookies but you can of course add in lots of different 'bits' for variety. One of our favourites is white chocolate chips and dried cranberries but just dark or milk chocolate chips are good too. You might also like to try crystallised ginger, micro fudge bits, fresh blueberries (these pop and go jammy), any dried fruit of your choice.

Comfort Cookies

Make~Life Easier Tip: *Just enjoy eating them!*

The Granola

Guest Recipe:

Tim's 'Just-Too-Tasty' Granola

My friend, Tim Lee (who owns a Nissan NV 200 campervan with his wife, Penny), has been making this granola for years and, for me it is the best home~made one around so – enjoy!

Ingredients (Makes lots)

- 500g jumbo oats

- 85g honey (tim says that some people prefer it sweeter so you might want to double-up on this is you have a sweet tooth)

- 60 ml peanut oil (also called groundnut oil)

- 2 tsp cinnamon

- 2½ tsp vanilla essence

- 100g additional ingredients (see below)

How to Prepare (Base Mix)

~ Mix the oats and cinnamon together in a large bowl

~ Gently heat the honey and oil in a small saucepan, stirring the mixture and keeping a close eye on it to ensure it doesn't boil.

~ Add the vanilla essence and mix well

~ Pour the hot mixture over the oats and mix thoroughly

~ Transfer to a large baking tray and bake in the oven for 20 to 30 minutes at 150°C

~ Stir the mix every five minutes to ensure that the edges don't overcook

~ When cooked, remove from the oven and allow to cool completely

~ Add your favourite additional ingredients and store in an airtight container

Additional ingredients

You can add whatever you like to the base mix and vary the amount depending on how rich you want your granola to be. Here a few ideas of what you can add:

• **chopped nuts** ~ brazil, almond, cashew, pistachio, walnut, hazelnut, pecan, peanuts

• **dried fruit** ~ raisins, currants, cranberries, sultanas, apricots, mango, apple, cherries, pear, blueberries

• coconut flakes, chopped preserved ginger, sunflower seeds, pumpkin seeds, sesame seeds

Variations:

o You can use other light, flavourless oils such as sunflower or rapeseed oil but olive oil is too heavy

o If you don't want to buy lots of individual packets of nuts or dried fruit use a packet of mixed dried fruit plus mixed nuts or trail mix.

o You can vary the sweeteners if you like maple syrup instead of honey or adding a tablespoon or two of muscovado sugar in place of some of the honey, which results in a darker mixture

o Roasting the nuts adds to their flavour and you can bake them yourself at the same time as cooking the oat mix. Just spread the nuts out on a baking tray and, like the oats, stir them frequently. Take them out when they turn a darker shade and begin to smell toasted. If you are cooking them on their own, you can increase the temperature to 175°C but keep a close eye on them as they burn very easily.

Tim's 'Just-Too-Tasty' Granola

Small Things That Make
a Big Difference

The Amazing 10-10 Chicken

This is an almost magical way to **cook up some chicken breasts** that you can then use in all sorts of recipes like: sandwiches, wraps, quesadillas, salads, side dishes. This method cooks the chicken in its own steam and juices so it stays lovely and moist and it is so quick and easy you won't believe it!

Ingredients (serves 2)

- 2 chicken breasts
- 1 tbsp. Of light oil

How to Cook

~ Put the oil in a frying over a low heat and move it around to coat the bottom

~ Place the two chicken breasts in the pan and cover with a lid or foil (see below for tip on the best lid to have)

~ Let the chicken cook on a medium heat for 10 minutes undisturbed (time it with your phone as the time is important)

~ Turn off the heat and let the chicken sit with the lid on for another 10 minutes

~ Take off the lid and your chicken is ready

You can use this method to cook fish as well and I recommend 7-7 minutes for a steaky piece of fish or 5-5 minutes for a thin, flat piece of fish. However always check that your meat or fish is cooked through before serving.

Watch Summer cook up some 10-10 Chicken on YouTube on The Camper Cookie channel:

https://www.youtube.com/watch?v=E0BM7V6WdPA

Yogam

'Yogam' (this is my word for it) is a lovely topping of yoghurt and cream for desserts, pancakes and as a special treat with your breakfast cereal. It has that luxury feel and taste of cream but it is healthier and I actually prefer it to plain cream now.

Ingredients (Serves 2-3)

- 4 heaped tbsp Greek yoghurt
- 2 heaped tbsp thick double cream

How to Prepare

~ Just mix the Greek yoghurt and cream in a bowl.

~ And that's it!

It is nice served with fruit. You can chop up some fruit (fresh or tinned) and add that to it.

Fruits that work really well are: blueberries, strawberries, raspberries, banana, tinned mango, tinned peaches but experiment and find out what floats your boat.

Check out my 'Fruit Yogam' recipe in 'Desserts' – I warn you, it's addictive!

Make~Life~Easier Tip: *If you make some Fruit Sticks for dessert on the BBQ for supper make a little extra and add this and some Yogam to your granola the next day. Oh my!*

Mayog

'Mayog' (this is my word for it) is a combination of mayonnaise and yoghurt that is a really useful base for making sauces that you can have with your BBQ food or add to sandwiches, wraps and pitta pockets. It is also healthier than mayonnaise alone as it reduces the fat and ups the protein as well as getting some helpful probiotics from the yoghurt. It is important to use Greek yoghurt as other yoghurts can be too runny.

Ingredients

- Greek yoghurt
- mayonnaise

How to Prepare

~ Just mix half Greek yoghurt to half mayonnaise in a bowl.

~ Add your flavouring e.g. sweet chilli sauce, mango chutney, barbeque sauce

Check out my 'BBQ Sauce's recipes in 'Lunches/Suppers'.

Salad Dressings

SALAD DRESSING 1: Honey & Mustard Dressing

Ingredients

- 50ml white wine vinegar
- 200ml extra virgin olive oil
- 1 tsp (heaped) Dijon mustard
- 1 tsp (heaped) course~grain mustard
- 3 tbsp runny honey
- 1 tbsp (heaped) soft, brown sugar

How to Prepare

~ Put the vinegar in a glass measuring jug

~ Mix the mustards in to the vinegar

~ Slowly add the olive oil while whisking

~ Add the runny honey while whisking

~ Add the sugar and mix to dissolve

SALAD DRESSING 2: Raspberry Vinaigrette

Ingredients

- 100g of ripe fresh raspberries (or you can use frozen)
- 2 tbsp cider vinegar
- 2 tbsp orange juice
- 3 tbsp olive oil
- 1 tbsp runny honey

How to Prepare

~ Mash up the raspberries with the vinegar

~ Add the orange juice, honey and oil and whisk together with a hand whisk

~ Season with salt and pepper to taste

Don't Forget...

These recipes are not only great for your camping life. They are really good for quick and easy Weekday Suppers too, when you just don't have the time for anything fancy but still want to eat good food. So make life just one long camping trip....

Happy Camping and Happy Eating!

About the Author

Summer is a passionate campervanner who also loves good food and she now blogs and writes books about the easy, home~style recipes that she creates for the campervan life.

New Campervan

Summer and her partner, Glyn, had been camping for many years but got fed up with putting up a tent in the half-light on a Friday night or taking it down in the rain at the end of a wet weekend so decided to buy themselves a small campervan. They went to the campervan shows but realised that their very small budget would buy them barely more than a wheel there! But then they found a company that sold converted Toyota Previas for a reasonable price and their new campervan, 'Trev-the-Prev' came in to their life.

Nutritious Food is Important

Summer had Chronic Fatigue Syndrome for many years but healed herself by researching, like a maniac, everything to do with mind-body health. She realised that nutritious food is very important to staying well and happy but found that it was not so easy to cook good food in the limited kitchen that you get in a small campervan. So she started to search for and develop easy, real-food recipes that they could cook when they were out having adventures.

Shares Her Recipes in Her Blog

She loves to share her recipes so she started up a blog (www.thecampercookie.com) and also writes recipe books for campervan cooking. She also demonstrates her recipes on YouTube (search 'the camper cookie') and at shows.

One Last Thing...

If you enjoyed this book or found it useful I'd be very grateful if you'd post a short review on Amazon. Your support really does make a difference and I read all the reviews personally so I can get your feedback and make this book even better.
Thanks again for your support!

Printed in Great Britain
by Amazon

33377732R00086